LET'S VISIT AUSTRALIA

Let's visit
AUSTRALIA

JOHN C. CALDWELL

BURKE

First published in Great Britain April 1965
Revised and reprinted October 1966
Revised and reprinted February 1968
New edition July 1971
Revised and reprinted May 1975
Third revised edition 1983

ACKNOWLEDGEMENTS

The publishers are grateful to the following for permission to reproduce copyright photographs in this book:
    The Australian News and Information Bureau in London; Robert Estall;
    Pan-American World Airlines; Paul Popper Ltd.
and to Garry Lyle for assistance in preparing this edition.

CIP data
Caldwell, John C.
    Let's visit Australia—3rd rev ed.
    1. Australia—Social life and customs—Juvenile
    literature
    I. Title
    994.06'3   DU107
    ISBN   0   222   00910   1

Burke Publishing Company Limited
Pegasus House, 116–120 Golden Lane, London EC1Y 0TL, England.
Burke Publishing (Canada) Limited
Toronto, Ontario, Canada.
Burke Publishing Company Inc.
540 Barnum Avenue, Bridgeport, Connecticut 06608, U.S.A.
Printed in Singapore by Tien Wah Press (Pte) Ltd.

Contents

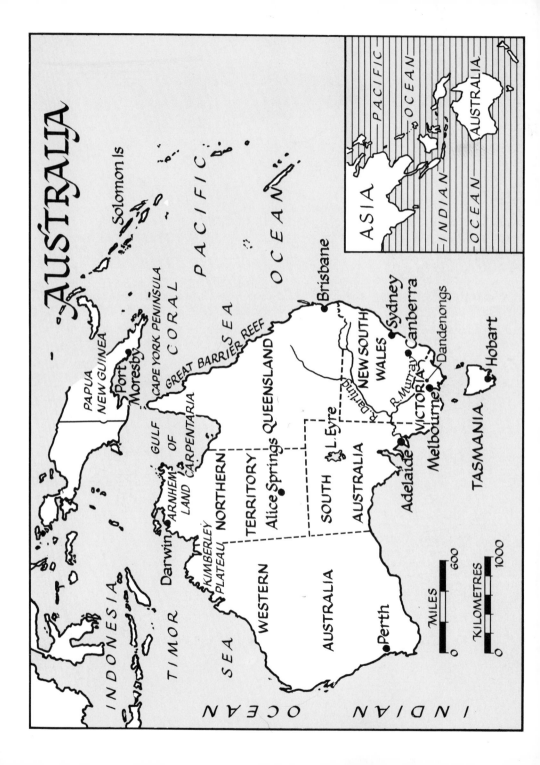

AUSTRALIA

Solomon Is

PAPUA NEW GUINEA

Port Moresby

PACIFIC OCEAN

CAPE YORK PENINSULA

CORAL SEA

GREAT BARRIER REEF

GULF OF CARPENTARIA

ARNHEM LAND

Darwin

KIMBERLEY PLATEAU

NORTHERN TERRITORY

Alice Springs

QUEENSLAND

Brisbane

NEW SOUTH WALES

Sydney
Canberra

Dandenongs

Darling

R. Murray

VICTORIA

Melbourne

SOUTH AUSTRALIA

L. Eyre

Adelaide

WESTERN AUSTRALIA

Perth

TASMANIA

Hobart

INDONESIA

TIMOR SEA

INDIAN OCEAN

PACIFIC OCEAN

MILES 600

KILOMETRES 1000

ASIA

PACIFIC OCEAN

INDIAN OCEAN

AUSTRALIA

Let's Visit Australia

The continent of Australia lies entirely south of the equator. Because of its position on the globe, Australia is often called the Land Down Under. There are many unusual facts about this country. It is one of the world's largest in area but among the smallest in population, and four-fifths of this population are crowded into a few cities. It is the only country to occupy a whole continent. Australia is the smallest continent in area, but it is the oldest.

Because of its age, Australia has animals and birds found nowhere else in the world. The continent became separated from the other land masses of the earth millions of years ago. Some varieties of birds and animals developed after Australia's formation as a separate continent.

Australia is the home of the kangaroo—or, rather, kangaroos. There are about forty different members of this group of animals. The kangaroos are found only in Australia (except for a tree-climbing species, found also in New Guinea). There are some very small members of this family, but the "big red" and

A kangaroo carrying its young. Kangaroos are found only in Australia and New Guinea, although today they can be seen in zoos throughout the world

the "great grey" kangaroos may stand higher than a man. Kangaroos are members of an ancient group of animals known as the *marsupials*. This word comes from a Latin word meaning "pouch". Members of this mammal family carry their young in a pouch.

The marsupials were a common group of mammals during the period when dinosaurs roamed the earth. Other more advanced types of mammals developed after the Australian continent was cut off from other land masses. It is interesting that the only other marsupials in the world are found in North America. These mammals did not develop elsewhere, or they died out as did the dinosaurs. The common opossum of North America is the only other member of the marsupials to survive.

8

Kangaroos did not have to compete for food with the hoofed animals such as the antelope and deer, bison and elk that developed elsewhere. Having no natural enemies, the kangaroo family thrived and developed into many species. We will read more about these unusual animals in another part of this book.

Because Australia was cut off from the rest of the world, it has remained almost a natural zoo for primitive animals that either disappeared or never developed elsewhere. There is one animal called the platypus which has a bill like a duck and lays eggs. There are strange birds that cannot fly; or which, instead of sitting on their eggs until the eggs hatch, bury the eggs and let the heat of decaying leaves do the job. There are many brightly coloured parrots, parakeets and other members of the parrot family of birds.

Australia is the home of the *boomerang*, a weapon that was invented long ago and from which we have a word often used in the English language. Made of wood, the boomerang—or rather, some kinds of boomerang—when thrown will return to the thrower. Boomerangs are still in use among the small number of aborigines who continue to live tribal lives. This brings us to another unusual fact about the Land Down Under. Its dark-skinned aborigines, or first human inhabitants, are considered to be the most primitive people in the world.

Before we learn about the geography and climate of Australia, let's review these unusual facts.

. . . Australia is the oldest continent, and it is also the smallest.

. . . Australia was the last continent to be discovered by

9

Europeans and the last to be settled by them. Because of its geological age, it has varieties of animals and birds that have either long since disappeared or never developed on other parts of the earth.

. . . Australia is the only country in the world to occupy an entire continent. It is one of the few countries which, instead of being overcrowded, has sought new citizens to fill its great empty spaces.

Let's read about the geography and climate of this interesting country.

The Land Down Under

Australia lies between the Indian Ocean and the Pacific Ocean. The northern part of the continent is about 750 miles (1,200 kilometres) south of the equator. The area is 2,967,741 square miles (about 7,500,000 square kilometres), almost the size of the continental United States. This makes Australia the sixth

The northern part of Australia is tropical. Coconut palms like this one are a familiar sight there

largest country in area. But with about 15,000,000 people, it is one of the smaller countries in population.

Let's look at the map so we will know where Australia is located. It is, of course, the world's smallest continent and, as we have said, it lies between the Indian and Pacific oceans, south-east of Asia. Many islands lie between northern Australia and Asia. Most of these islands belong to Indonesia. The Timor (pronounced TEE-more) Sea separates Australia from the Indonesian islands. New Guinea, the world's second largest island, lies directly north of Australia. It is separated from Australia by the Arafura Sea and the Torres Strait.

North-east of Australia is a part of the Pacific Ocean called the Coral Sea. The Solomon Islands, where many World War II battles were fought, are among the many islands in the Coral Sea. To the east there are only coral reefs and a few small islands. The Dominion of New Zealand, which has close ties of culture and common interest with Australia, lies 1,200 miles (1,920 kilometres) south-east of Australia across a part of the Pacific Ocean called the Tasman Sea.

The Indian and Pacific oceans meet along the south coast of Australia. The map shows us there is one large island south of mainland Australia. It is called Tasmania and is one of the six states making up the Commonwealth of Australia.

West of Australia there are only a few small islands between that continent and Africa. The map shows us that the land nearest Australia is New Guinea to the north. At the closest point, it is only about 150 miles (240 kilometres) from Australia.

Long, long ago, the continent was probably connected to these islands. But it was long ago indeed. Geologists estimate that Australia's rocks were formed more than 500 million years ago.

The northern tip of Australia is about 750 miles (1,200 kilometres) from the equator. This fact and the fact that Australia lies south of the equator should tell us something about the climate. Part of the continent lies within the Torrid Zone and has a hot or tropical climate. The Torrid Zone includes parts of the world between the Tropic of Cancer north of the equator and the Tropic of Capricorn south of the equator. About one third of Australia lies within the tropics. The extreme northern fringes are monsoonal—regular, heavy summer rainfall, with very little rain for the rest of the year.

The fact that Australia lies south of the equator tells us something else about its weather and climate. In all parts of the world south of the equator, seasons are the reverse of those north of the equator. Australia's summer begins in December; wintertime begins in June.

Along the northern coasts, and particularly in north-eastern Queensland, is tropical jungle and rain forest. The average temperature in such regions may be more than 80° Fahrenheit (27° Centigrade) and the average rainfall is very high, too. In summer the air is very humid and the wearing of clothes a discomfort. There are some large crocodile-infested rivers. Many of these regularly overflow their banks during the wet season to flood vast areas of the surrounding land; yet in winter they may dry to little more than a series of pools.

13

Inland from the northern coast and extending for vast distances is a wild, dry and desolate land. I have travelled by air from Sydney to Darwin, the only city in the north of the Northern Territory. Looking down from the plane, sometimes you see not a sign of human habitation for 100 miles (160 kilometres). There are great areas of sand, rock and clay. Here and there are trees, but for the most part the vegetation consists of bushes that can grow with very little water. Australians call this part of their country the Never-Never. There are places in the middle of the continent where rivers flow inland instead of toward the sea. There are large areas without water, yet underground there may be huge natural stores known as artesian

Australian cattle by a dam

Ayers Rock, in the Northern Territory, often called "the world's largest pebble"

basins. In fact, many sheep- and cattle-grazing areas rely heavily on such water, which is brought to the surface by windmill and stored in tanks.

The map shows us some names given to this part of Australia. The Great Sandy Desert is in north-west Australia, and the Great Victoria Desert is in southern Australia. There are lakes and rivers, but most of these are dry much of the year. Some rivers flow for a short distance, then sink into the ground. In Western Australia there is a large lake. Its name tells us something about the feeling of the pioneers who explored the Out-

15

back (the more remote and sparsely populated regions of Australia). The name is Lake Disappointment.

It is in part because the middle of the continent is dry that Australia has a very small population. There are some ranches or *stations*, as these ranches are called, scattered through the Outback. There are a few aborigines. And, no matter how dry it may be, or how little vegetation there is (except in the most extreme of drought conditions), there are kangaroos, wallabies and other members of the kangaroo family.

Two thirds of Australia lies within the Temperate Zone. A chain of mountains, known as the Great Dividing Range, extends from north to south along the east coast and, although interrupted by Bass Strait, continues in Tasmania. Different parts of the Range bear different names. Inland from Sydney lie the Blue Mountains. Another section in the south-east is called the Snowy Mountains. These form part of the Australian Alps, the highest section of the Great Dividing Range.

The Great Dividing Range separates the rolling hills and sometimes fertile plains of the eastern coastal area from the drier lands of the interior. South or east of the mountains there is plenty of rainfall. The vast plains to the west, while drier, are excellent for sheep and cattle grazing and for wheat growing. Considerable areas now irrigated produce fruit, rice and cotton. Further west the country falls gradually into a huge arid basin dominated by salt lakes which are mostly dry. Some parts of these are well below sea-level. Still further west we come again to desert plateau, barren rolling hills and finally the

16

Australia's mountain areas provide pleasant winter sports centres, as well as hydro-electric power. Here is a ski class in progress

Great Victoria Desert and Great Sandy Desert of inland Western Australia.

Most of Australia's population and rich farmlands are located down the Queensland coast, through New South Wales (but excluding its far western reaches) through most of Victoria and into south-eastern South Australia. Tasmania and the south-western part of Western Australia are well-settled segments cut off from the rest—Tasmania by sea and Western Australia by desert. The biggest cities and richest farmlands are in the south-eastern corner of the continent.

Let's look now at rainfall in Australia's big cities. Brisbane on the north-east coast averages 45 inches (114 centimetres). Sydney, farther south on the east coast, has 48 inches (122 centimetres); Melbourne and Adelaide on the south coast have 26 inches (66 centimetres) and 21 inches (53 centimetres). Perth, the largest city in Western Australia, has about 35 inches (89 centimetres) of rain each year.

Along the southern and eastern coasts where Australia's big cities are located, temperatures are similar to those of the Mediterranean—very hot in the summer, quite cold in the winter. As we have said, the seasons are the reverse of seasons in Europe.

During the Australian winter, there is snow on some of the mountains. On Mt. Kosciusko, Mt. Buller, Mt. Hotham and Mt. Buffalo and the mountains of Tasmania, snowfall is heavy enough for good skiing.

There are two other interesting features of Australia's geography. First, let's mention the fine ocean beaches. Along the east and parts of the south and west coasts are hundreds of beaches. The surf is unusually high, and surfboarding has become one of Australia's important sports. The coast of Queensland, in eastern Australia, is famous as a winter holiday region

Part of the underwater observatory at Green Island, on the Barrier Reef

A view of Green Island

because of its sunshine and mild climate. The most popular part is the Gold Coast, near Brisbane.

The second unusual geographic feature is also found along the east and north-east coast. The largest coral reef in the world extends from north of Brisbane all the way to New Guinea. Called the Great Barrier Reef, it extends for 1,250 miles (2,000 kilometres) and covers 80,000 square miles (about 200,000 square kilometres). There are numerous beautiful tropical islands scattered along the reef, or between the reef and the mainland. There are coral gardens, filled with beautifully coloured tropical fish, strange green sea turtles and very big sharks.

Coral reefs are found throughout the South Pacific. Coral is formed from the dead bodies of tiny sea creatures called polyps. The combined skeletons of millions of polyps are deposited on the bottom of the ocean and slowly build upward until the coral reaches the surface. A coral reef may be quite close to the shore or a long distance away from it. It protects the coast from the force of the ocean waves. This makes the water between the reef and the shore calm. The calm waters inside the reef are clear, and it is possible to look down and see tropical fish and other creatures clearly.

As we have said, the Great Barrier Reef is the largest coral reef in the world. There are holiday resorts on the islands; there are swimming beaches; and everywhere there are places where skin divers can easily see and dive to collect coral, fish and other creatures of the tropical ocean.

The Murray River and its tributaries form one of the longest river systems in the world, but the Murray River itself is the only one which is navigable for any great distance. The Murray-Murrumbidgee-Darling system drains the south-eastern part of Australia and flows into the Great Australian Bight near Adelaide.

Now let's look at the map once more to learn about the division of Australia into states and territories. Beginning in the north-east is Queensland, with an area of 667,000 square miles (about 1,727,000 square kilometres) and about 2,400,000 population. Brisbane is the capital. South of Queensland is New South Wales with an area of 309,433 square miles (about 800,000 square kilometres) and a population of about 5,500,000. This is the largest state in population; and Sydney, its capital, with over 3,000,000 people, is Australia's largest city.

The state of Victoria, with a population of about 4,000,000, lies south of New South Wales. It has an area of 87,884 square miles (about 228,000 square kilometres), and its capital city is Melbourne, with nearly 3 million people. South Australia (380,070 square miles—984,380 square kilometres) is west of Victoria and has about $1\frac{1}{2}$ million people. Adelaide, the capital, has a population of about one million. Western Australia is often called "The Western Third" of the continent. It has an area of nearly one million square miles (about $2\frac{1}{2}$ million square kilometres) and a population of about 1,300,000. Perth, the state capital, has about 900,000 people.

Tasmania, Australia's baby state, has an area of 26,215 square miles (about 67,000 square kilometres) and a population of 430,000. Hobart, the capital, has about 200,000 inhabitants.

Canberra, the national capital, has almost all of the population of about 250,000 people contained within the Federal Capital Territory of 939 square miles (about 2,400 square kilometres) which is part of south-eastern New South Wales.

The map shows us that a large part of Australia is called the Northern Territory. Though not one of the six Australian states, the Northern Territory now governs itself through its own elected parliament, called the Legislative Assembly. It has a population of about 123,000, including about 30,000 part- and full-blooded aborigines.

Much of Australia's dry, wild Outback lies in the Northern Territory. Large areas used to be called Native Reserves and are set aside for the aborigine tribes.

Tribesmen from New Guinea's mountains. The man on the right is the village government representative. The cap is his badge of office

Finally, let's mention Australia's overseas territories. Until recently, the best-known of these territories was Papua New Guinea, a country occupying the eastern half of the huge island 150 miles (240 kilometres) north of Australia. However, Papua New Guinea is no longer an Australian territory. Though it still receives a good deal of Australian help, it is now a fully independent, self-governing country, and a member of the United Nations Organisation.

During World War II great naval battles and bitter jungle fighting took place in Papua New Guinea and the Solomon Islands. The defeat of the Japanese in this area was a turning point in the war and perhaps saved Australia from invasion.

Many tribes in the interior of Papua New Guinea are very primitive. The area includes wild, jungle-covered mountains that either remain largely unexplored or are seldom entered by Government patrol officers. There are also tribes which may still from time to time, although they know it is forbidden, indulge in a little head-hunting! Before the country came under Australian influence there was constant warfare between different tribes. The people of Papua New Guinea speak hundreds of different languages.

There are several small South Pacific islands belonging to Australia. Norfolk Island lies in the South Pacific Ocean almost directly east of Brisbane. With an area of only 13·5 square miles (about 35 square kilometres) and a population of

A view of one of the rivers flowing through the Owen Stanley Ranges in Papua. In these mountains the Japanese army was defeated for the first time in the Second World War

about 1,500, it is famous for a variety of pine tree that has been introduced to other parts of the Pacific.

Australian islands in the Indian Ocean include the Cocos-Keeling Islands located north-west of Australia and Christmas Island, south of Java in Indonesia. Finally, Australia claims about 2,350,000 square miles (about 6,100,000 square kilometres) of territory in the Antarctic. Except for scientists and explorers, no one lives in this land of ice and snow.

If we were to look at a large-scale map of Australia, we would notice many strange-sounding names of towns, rivers and mountains. There would be names like Woomera, Wallaroo and Wagga Wagga which come from the language of Australia's aborigines or first known human inhabitants. The "Abos", as they are often called, were, and in some areas still are, the most primitive people on earth.

Let's read now about these strange people who migrated to Australia thousands of years before it was discovered by Europeans.

The Aborigines

The word *aborigine* means the first inhabitant of a country. The Indians of North America were the aborigines living on that continent when Europeans discovered, explored and settled the United States.

The aboriginal people of Australia are a distinctive race called Australoids, thought to be related to the Dravidians of India. The Dravidians were a dark-skinned people who lived

Australian aborigines. The man on the left is holding two boomerangs

in India before the Aryan or white invaders came to that country over 4,000 years ago.

When the Europeans began to settle Australia, the aborigines were as primitive as any people on earth. And there are still aborigines scattered through the great empty middle of Australia who have not changed in any way and who live exactly as did their forefathers thousands of years ago. Yet, though these aborigines who live in what is called the old tribal manner are considered the world's most primitive people, they have developed senses and abilities that are probably not possessed by any other people.

It is estimated that there are now more than 160,000 aborigines and part-aborigines in Australia, and their numbers are increasing. About half now live in towns or cities, while the rest live and work on the great cattle and sheep stations in the interior, or on their own lands. Those who are educated speak good English, but some still speak what is called *pidgin* English. This is English that may be mixed with some aboriginal words and always English that is very simple and without correct grammar. When I was travelling in the Northern Territory, the driver of my car wanted to know the name of an aborigine man. He asked, "You fella what name?"

Almost 20 per cent of the aborigines live in the Northern Territory. Since 1976 these have become the legal and permanent owners of about 150,000 square miles (390,000 square kilometres) of Northern Territory land, including the huge area which used to be called Native Reserves.

Aborigines preparing to take part in a traditional tribal dance—a *corroboree*

Aborigines who live in a tribal state usually wear little or no clothing. For the most part, a *naga* or loincloth is the only article of clothing. The primitive aborigines have weapons and tools of a kind, but have never learned to grow any crops, and have only a very elementary system of numbers and counting. They do not live in villages. Usually a family live more or less isolated from the rest of the tribe, with only the most primitive form of bough shelter, called a *wurlie*.

Some families live in areas where there is almost no rain. Often they may live in areas called *salt flats*. This is the term given to parts of the Outback where all soil is gone. The surface of the ground is almost like rock. Usually the only vegetation is the saltbush and the bluebush.

The aborigine's wife is called his *lubra*. Along with the children, a family group usually has several dogs. When fire is needed, the man or his lubra make it by rubbing sticks together. The meat they eat is relatively uncooked by our standards. Food is so scarce that everything that moves must be considered food. For example, some kinds of ants rich in a honey-like fluid may be eaten. There are small animals in the bush, too. Rats, an occasional kangaroo, birds and a few wild plants make up the aborigine diet.

In order to survive, the tribal aborigines have developed unusual senses and abilities. They have uncanny abilities in tracking and in finding water.

Australian aborigines have the finest eyesight of any people on earth. They are the very best trackers. A hunter can follow the tracks of a kangaroo or other animal that may have been made days before and yet track down the animal. Also the aborigines of the Outback developed the world's strangest hunting weapon—the boomerang.

There are several varieties of boomerangs and another weapon called a *woomera* is also used by the aborigines. Some boomerangs are made to return to the thrower, but others do not come back. The typical hunting boomerang is made to hit its target and does not return. The boomerang will hit one animal, then bounce away to hit another.

Boomerangs are used to kill large animals like kangaroos. A

An aboriginal boy

boomerang can also be thrown into a flock of birds and kill several.

The woomera is a holder for a spear. Using the holder, aborigines can throw spears great distances and with great accuracy. In olden days, woomeras and spears were the aborigines' main fighting weapons. Now they are used only for hunting the larger kinds of kangaroo, or in tribal ceremonies and dances.

Aborigine boys are given toy boomerangs when they are three or four years old. The boys learn how to use the weapon but are not allowed to throw a real boomerang until they are initiated into young manhood.

The boomerang has been described as a fascinating toy and a deadly weapon. For this reason, aborigine parents do not allow boys to use the real weapon until they know exactly how it is to be used.

It is the aim of the Australian government to educate and train aborigines until they are in every way like other citizens. Generally, they now have the same rights as all other Australians, although in some areas they find it hard to obtain them fully. Proper schools have been set up for the education of almost all aboriginal children.

Not only are government schools provided where enough children can be gathered together, but various Christian missions have long been established to provide not only schooling but health and other services.

In Arnhem Land, a part of the Northern Territory, many aborigines still wear the naga loincloth. Others dress in clothing like that worn by Americans, Europeans or other Australians. Most small children wear no clothes.

A Visit to the Daly River

When I was in northern Australia I spent a day visiting the Daly River Native Reserve. This is the second largest reserve in the Northern Territory and is not very far—by Australian standards—from the Northern Territory's capital, Darwin. Strictly speaking, these huge tracts of the Northern Territory should not now be called Reserves since they are no longer owned by the Australian government but by the aborigines who live in them. However, that change happened very recently and has not, so far, made much difference to the old Daly River Reserve.

So empty is this part of Australia that I had to drive for over an hour before reaching the first tiny settlement south of Darwin. Then for another 75 miles (120 kilometres) the road wound through a cattle station. In all this distance, there was not one house. But everywhere there were kangaroos, wallabies, wild buffaloes, wild pigs and the beautiful wild horses of northern Australia, called *brumbies*.

The aborigines' land lies along the banks of the Daly River where there are huge crocodiles to be found. Two Catholic mis-

31

sionaries, and a policeman and his wife live here with the aborigines. The policeman and the missionaries have two-way radios. Each week a small plane lands in a clearing in the bush to bring supplies, mail and medicine.

All through the Australian Bush and Outback country, people use two-way radios just as we might use telephones. Children "go to school" by radio, talking to a teacher who may be in a school far away. The radio is used in case of sickness or other emergency. A Flying Doctor Service provides medical help. Doctors prescribe over the radio; if someone is very ill, the Flying Doctor comes in a small plane. There are little landing strips all through the bush.

In addition to the many animals and birds of the bush, there are snakes, lizards and interesting insects. There are magnetic anthills, too, sometimes as high as sixteen feet (five metres). Each anthill is built exactly in a north-south position. If you

These aborigines live in a reserve—note their clothes as compared with the dress of their tribal cousins

are lost in the northern bush country, you need only find a magnetic anthill to find north! The anthills are called "magnetic" because they point to the north like the needle of a compass.

On the Daly River land, family groups live in the way we have already described. Some of the men earn money by making boomerangs which are sent to the cities and sold to tourists.

They also still follow some ancient customs. There are primitive dances and ceremonies, called *corroborees*, to a chanted accompaniment of strange-sounding songs. Every year, usually during the rainy season, aborigines disappear from their reserves, from the sheep and cattle stations where many work. Called the annual *walkabout*, this period may cover three months. The aborigines usually cast off their civilised clothing, and walk long distances through desert and bush.

The Australians have a saying that the aborigines are hungry for "bush tucker". When they do return from the walkabout, people are much thinner but are happy to resume their normal way of living. No one really knows what takes place during a walkabout, or how far the aborigines travel from their homes. This is one of the strange mysteries of the Australian bush country.

It is interesting that of the 30,000 aborigines living in the Northern Territory, less than half are employed in full-time jobs. This is because the people are slow to change or to learn

This man comes from the Australian desert. He lives on a mission but is free to go on a walkabout whenever he chooses

new ways of doing things. The attitude of white Australians towards the black Abos has changed in recent years. I noticed that the few white citizens of the Daly River had respect for the unusual abilities of the aborigines.

The aborigines themselves are usually very friendly to white visitors but they have not always been so. Though armed only with boomerang and woomera, they often attacked pioneers in the early days. However, it must be remembered that the pioneers were invading their territory, endangering their food supplies. Moreover, the pioneers often treated them brutally. The highway leading south from Darwin to Alice Springs is named after John McDouall Stuart, first man to cross

34

the continent. Stuart began his explorations of the bush country in 1858, and in 1862 he won a prize of £2,000 offered by the government for the first man to cross the centre of the continent from south to north. Stuart did not win his prize easily.

On June 27, 1860, Stuart wrote in his diary that he had reached a place in the middle of the continent but was turning back. He wrote:

> . . . my party is far too small to cope with such wily and determined natives as those we have just encountered. With such as these as our enemies in our rear, and most probably, far worse in advance, it would be destruction to all my party for me to attempt to go on.

There is a small and usually dry creek on the map of the Northern Territory marking the place where Stuart made this entry in his diary. It is still known as Attack Creek. But Stuart tried again; and two years later, in 1862, he won the prize for being the first to cross the continent through the centre.

About Explorers and Pioneers

The earliest recorded discovery of Australia was by the Dutch ship *Duyfken*, which followed the west coast of Cape York Peninsula in 1606. During the seventeenth century, other Dutch ships going to and from the Dutch settlements in the East Indies also reached Australia from time to time.

In 1642 Captain Abel Tasman, one of the greatest of the Dutch explorers, proved that Australia was either an island or a continent and not a part of the Antarctic continent. Tasman went on to discover New Zealand. Tasmania, Australia's island state, and the Tasman Sea, the part of the Pacific between Australia and New Zealand, are named after him.

An Englishman, William Dampier, visited the north-west coast in 1688. But the man most responsible for Australia's settlement was Captain James Cook who landed near the present city of Sydney in 1770. Captain Cook was one of the great explorers of the Pacific. He reached Australia after having mapped the coast of New Zealand. Captain Cook's ship, the *Endeavour*, sailed into Botany Bay near Sydney in April of 1770. He claimed the new land for Great Britain and named it New South Wales.

There is an interesting relationship between the American colonies and Australia. Captain Cook's visit took place a few years before the American Revolution. At the time England was too busy in North America to worry about faraway Australia. It was only after the American colonies had won their

36

freedom that England began to be interested in New South Wales. Many convicts had earlier been sent to the American colonies. England became interested in Australia because a new place was needed to which to send convicts.

New South Wales was suggested, and in 1788 the first settlement of convicts was founded by Captain Arthur Phillip on the bay where Sydney is now located. Captain Phillip described Sydney Harbour as "the finest harbour in the world". During the next four years Phillip and his convicts had a difficult time. They had to struggle against starvation.

In 1790 John Macarthur arrived from England. In 1797 he bought eight merino sheep from a ship's captain and began to breed a flock. Australia now has more sheep than any nation on earth, and its great sheep and wool industry began with Macarthur's eight merinos.

However, for many years most of the settlers arriving in Australia were convicts. In 1813 the Blue Mountains, inland from Sydney, were explored and crossed. This opened up new grazing land and brought new settlers. In the 1850s, gold was discovered in New South Wales and in the present state of Victoria. Soon people were pouring into Australia. In 1892–3 gold was discovered at Coolgardie and Kalgoorlie in Western Australia; a few years later more gold was discovered. Each time the news of a gold strike reached England, thousands of people jammed the ships offering passage to Australia.

Tasmania was among the first areas opened to free settlement. In part, this was because the British feared that either

The first European explorers to reach Australia made their way across country like this

the French or the Dutch might become interested in Australia. A few settlements were made along the hot coast of north Australia for the same reason, but these were soon abandoned.

Melbourne, now Australia's second city, was founded in 1835 by free settlers led by John Pascoe Fawkner and John Batman. In 1842 the Melbourne area was opened to free settlement.

The determined settlers began to expand their frontiers. Not only was Melbourne growing as a manufacturing centre but explorers—often with farmers close behind them, eager for new sheep and cattle pastures—pushed into the unknown areas of the continent. But their efforts were not rewarded. Most of the interior was without water. The great inland sea which many thought must exist proved to be mythical. A. C. Gregory (north Australia 1855–6), Burke and Wills (who were the first to cross the continent from south to north, 1860–61), F. G. Gregory (north-western Australia 1861), P. E. Warburton (north-western Australia 1872–3) and John Forrest (who crossed the continent from west to east, 1874) were amongst explorers who, like John McDouall Stuart, mentioned earlier, confirmed the sad fact that here was an "inside-out" continent: its best lands were around its coasts.

Camels were introduced as an aid to exploration, and their descendants are still found in some parts of central Australia. Numerous explorers died from thirst and starvation, were killed by the aborigines or simply disappeared without a trace.

The task of building a telegraph line began in 1870, and the line was completed in 1872. Beginning at Adelaide in South Australia, the telegraph line crosses 1,973 miles (nearly 3,200 kilometres) of bush, desert and jungle to Darwin. There it connected with underwater cables so that Australia had direct communications with the rest of the world.

Building the "O.T"—as it is still called—across virtually unknown country was a tremendous achievement. The hot climate is so extreme that it may make a man's hair stop growing. It is usually so dry that the task of supplying water and food for working parties was enormous, quite apart from the colossal job of transporting the materials. The "O.T" stands as a monument to human courage and endurance.

There are many parts of the Australian Outback that look like the very worst areas crossed by American wagon trains taking settlers to the West. However, the heart of the continent is so dry, so hot, still so unexplored, that it is almost empty. We can understand why Australia, almost as large as the continental United States, has so few people. There are vast areas without water. There are deserts, areas of salt lake, scrub and bush.

In other sections of this book we will learn how Australia is trying to attract pioneers and about projects that will take water into areas of the Outback. With water, there are vast areas that can be opened to farming. We will learn more about the people who do live in the Outback. Much of Australia is still so wild and uninhabited that even the comfortable buses that take tourists from Adelaide to Alice Springs are equipped with two-way radios.

There is a railway from Adelaide to "The Alice", as the Australians call their largest town in the middle of the continent. The population of The Alice is about 12,000. From Alice Springs there is a bitumen highway to Darwin, capital of the Northern Territory.

The highway is named after Stuart, the man who first crossed this part of the continent. The distance from Alice Springs to Darwin is about 970 miles (1,552 kilometres). In all this distance there is only one town of any size: Tennant Creek. This has a population of about 1,000 and is the third largest town in the Northern Territory.

Australian Wildlife

Before we read about the cities of Australia, let's take a look at the wildlife. Captain Francis Pelsart, a Dutchman wrecked off the western coast of Australia in 1629, described in his journal a strange animal seen along the coast in great numbers. He wrote that the animal appeared to be "a species of cat, with a head resembling that of a civet cat, a long tail, and very short forepaws like those of a monkey. Its two hind legs, on the contrary, are upwards of half an ell in length and it walks on the flat of the heavy part of the leg . . . it sits on its hind legs, and clutches its food in its forepaws, just like a squirrel or monkey."

Captain Pelsart's description was so accurate that three hundred years later zoologists were able to identify the strange animal as the tammer wallaby, a small member of the kangaroo family found in Western Australia. The Dutchman had made the first authentic account of any member of this interesting family of animals.

We have learned that because of being separated from the rest of the world, Australia developed unusual forms of animals. The kangaroo family is but one of the interesting animal groups.

The Australian bush seems sometimes to be alive with colour and sound. At least 60 members of the parrot family are found in Australia. The cockatoos are the largest, some being as big as hawks. The galah (pink, grey or blue) is an attractive

This is a galah—one of the largest parrots found in Australia

A rosella, one of Australia's most colourful parrots

bird with a loud call, found throughout the continent and sometimes seen in flocks numbering thousands. The red-tailed black cockatoo is so large that it is difficult to believe that it is a parrot.

Also among the 60 known species of parrots are the beautiful rosella, the crimson and green king parrot, the superb parrot, and several smaller members of the parrot family called lorikeets.

Another attractive bird is the kookaburra, also known as the laughing jackass because of its strange, laughing call. Found throughout the continent, the kookaburra is probably Australia's most popular bird, and it is also a very useful one, because it kills poisonous snakes. I took a picture of a kookaburra which had perched on a chair in a front garden.

43

The kookaburra—it might be called the national bird of Australia

The animal most typical of Australian wildlife is the kangaroo. As we have said, there are more than 40 different varieties. 'Roos, as these animals are called in Australia, are found in every part of the continent.

Only the largest of the animals are properly called kangaroos. Those next in size, heavy-set hill animals, are wallaroos and euros. The middle-sized members are wallabies and tree kangaroos. Then come rock wallabies and pademelons, sometimes called scrub wallabies; and then the smallest varieties— rat kangaroos that are often no bigger than rabbits.

The best known of these many varieties is the great grey or forester kangaroo, found in open woods and bush country. This is the variety usually kept in zoos. A great grey can weigh up to 200 pounds (about 90 kilograms) and cover more than

44

25 feet (8 metres) in one jump. However, it can easily be outrun by a horse.

Kangaroos and wallabies are usually found in mobs, the word used by Australians and New Zealanders for any large group of animals. Farmers speak of a mob of sheep or cattle. Kangaroo mobs get up early to feed. By midday the bush seems empty because the animals find shady places to sleep and rest during the heat of the day. In late afternoon the bush becomes alive again as animals come out to feed. Many species of 'roos feed all night also.

Kangaroos are usually timid; but if cornered or wounded, a big boomer, as an old male is called, will fight and is dangerous. The long hind legs are powerful. Even the short front legs are used to hug dogs to death. One way kangaroos fight dogs is to wade into a stream, catch the dogs as they come into the water and drown them.

There is a sharp claw on the middle toe of each hind leg. This claw and the powerful hind leg can rip a dog or a human being to pieces. A kangaroo's tail is also a powerful weapon. When travelling at full speed the kangaroo carries its huge tail extended—a useful counterweight to its body.

When it is born, a baby kangaroo may be only one inch (just over two centimetres) long. It has no fur at this stage in life and looks rather like a worm. At once, the tiny blind baby finds its way to the mother's pouch and stays there while its body grows and takes the shape of a kangaroo. Now it is called a *joey*. After about three months, the joey begins to get out of the pouch and try its legs. But it goes back to the pouch until it is too big to fit there comfortably. Then its mother makes it stay out and learn to live like adult kangaroos.

The joey in the picture on page 8 is almost too big for his mother's pouch. This picture was taken in a game or wild-life sanctuary where animals are protected. Kangaroos are easily tamed; joeys make nice and friendly pets.

It is a surprise to know that there is no law to protect most varieties of kangaroos. There are men who make their living killing 'roos. The reason for this is that kangaroos are still so common in many parts of Australia that they eat grass that cattle or sheep should be eating. In addition, they are often a serious highway traffic problem. There are many parts of Australia away from the big cities where you will see thousands of kangaroos and wallabies in a day's drive.

Aborigines have always eaten 'roos. Kangaroo-tail soup is considered a delicacy by all Australians. In sparsely settled parts of the country, kangaroo or wallaby meat is an important source of food, and settlers speak of the animals as "hopping mutton".

We have mentioned that some men make their living killing kangaroos. Hunting by night with a powerful torch, a man may kill several hundred animals every night. The meat is sold to canneries for dog and cat food. Even though thousands of animals are killed in this way, and other thousands are killed on roads, kangaroos continue to be plentiful in some areas. However, it is feared that some species may already be extinct, and nature-lovers are concerned about the continuing slaughter. Unfortunately, kangaroos eat grass badly needed by cattle and sheep. For this reason most farmers consider the kangaroo an enemy.

Kangaroos are interesting animals, and there is much more we could write about them. But Australia has other animals we should learn about also. In the north there are big black wild buffaloes. And there are wild dogs called dingoes. There are two especially interesting animals, both of which are found only in Australia. These are the platypus, an animal that lays eggs, and the cuddly koala, which is probably the most lovable of all fur-bearing animals.

One of our pictures shows a koala (pronounced ko-AH-la) and her baby. These little animals are sometimes called native bears, but they are not bears at all. They are members of the marsupial family. Usually, a koala will eat only the leaves of certain species of eucalyptus (gum) tree which grow in the locality where it was born, and it cannot easily get used to

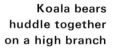

Koala bears huddle together on a high branch

A eucalyptus forest near Melbourne

eating leaves from other species or from other localities. Hence the koalas would certainly become extinct if they were not heavily protected by law, for they are completely defenceless. They are slow-moving tree dwellers but will walk from tree to tree.

One of our pictures shows a eucalyptus forest of the kind in which koalas live. This tree, called a *gum* in Australia, is native to that continent. Although its leaves are like those of other hardwood trees, it is an evergreen. The leaves are filled with an *aromatic* oil. This means that the leaves when crushed have a fragrant and pungent smell. Varieties of eucalyptus have been introduced to many other parts of the world.

The koalas were native to certain eucalyptus forests through-

48

out eastern and south-eastern Australia. Unfortunately, for many years the little animals were killed for their fine fur and are no longer abundant. Koalas are now protected, and wild koalas can be seen in areas near Melbourne. There is a koala zoo near Sydney where many of the little animals live almost as in a wild state. Koalas have one baby a year. After staying in the mother's pouch for several months, the baby koala rides on its mother's back for several more months before learning to care for itself.

The platypus (pronounced PLATTER-puss) is the strangest of all Australian mammals. It and another animal called the echidna (eh-KID-nuh) may be the last living links between reptiles and mammals. They are the only egg-laying mammals in the world.

The platypus is a shy animal, usually feeding at night. It has a mouth shaped like the flat bill of a duck and it feeds under water. The flat bill acts like a radar. The platypus swims with its eyes and ears closed! The radarlike bill tells the animal where worms and insects can be found. The little furry swimmer can stay under water for five minutes and is quite an acrobat in the water. The mother platypus lays a single egg in a burrow in the ground. After the egg hatches, the baby feeds on its mother's milk as do all other mammals.

The echidna is sometimes called the spiny anteater. It is covered with sharp spines, and has a tube-like mouth with a long tongue and no teeth. The egg of this strange animal is laid in the mother's pouch where it hatches.

Australia's strangest animal—the platypus

The echidna is found all over Australia, and the platypus in eastern Australia only. Both animals are now protected by law, and the platypus has become rare. It was hunted and trapped for its thick and beautiful fur.

As we have said, all of Australia is like a big outdoor zoo. Away from the big cities, one sees many varieties of interesting birds and animals. We do not have space in this book to tell about all the unusual wildlife. There are one or two flesh-eating marsupials. One variety, now scarce, is called the Tasmanian devil; another is called the tiger cat.

50

Finally we should mention the wombat. A full-grown wombat is about three feet (over 90 centimetres) long. These animals have their homes at the ends of long tunnels dug into banks. Wombat tunnels are sometimes nine feet long (about three metres) and create problems. The deep tunnels cause embankments to crumble.

Australia is the home of the second largest bird in the world. Called the emu, this big bird looks much like an ostrich and cannot fly. A full-grown emu is nearly as tall as a man. The female lays eight or nine eggs, and the male is given the job of sitting on the eggs and protecting the chicks when they hatch. Once common, the emu is now found only inland where there

The wombat which lives in a deep burrow at the end of a long tunnel

An emu—it is really
a bird with
undeveloped wings

is still uninhabited and open country. It is Australia's national
bird and, like the national animal—the kangaroo—it has a
place in the Australian coat-of-arms.

Among other birds are the black swans, found only in
Australia, and a group of birds called the megapodes or mound
birds. We might call members of this bird family the laziest of
all birds. They do not sit on their eggs. Instead, they cover their
eggs with a big mound of earth and decaying leaves. The
warmth of the decaying vegetable matter hatches the eggs so
that the mother mound bird does not have to spend hours every
day sitting on her eggs.

Two other interesting Australian birds are the lyrebird and
the fairy penguin. The lyrebird is found in no other part of the
world. The bird has a huge tail which is spread out in the shape

of the musical instrument called a lyre (pronounced like *liar*). The male bird's tail may be three feet (one metre) long. The lyrebird is the largest and most unusual songbird in the world. This bird can sing beautifully; also it can mimic any sound. It can bark like a dog or even make a sound like a portable power saw!

There are many seabirds along the Australian coasts. Each year thousands of people visit Phillip Island, near Melbourne, to watch the penguin parade. The fairy penguin is a member of a family of flightless seabirds. Each day the little fairy penguins swim far out to sea to feed. In late afternoon the penguins return to their nesting burrows on Phillip Island. As the hundreds of neat black and white penguins reach the beach, they take formation like a human army and march into the low hills where the nesting burrows are located.

Remember the surprise of the Dutch sea captain when he first saw members of the kangaroo family? The early settlers throughout Australia must have been surprised often by the strange birds and animals, so different from anything found in their homelands. Perhaps it was because everything was different that the settlers sent home for a few varieties of birds common in England.

Unfortunately, their choice of birds was not very good. If you were to visit the temperate parts of Australia, you would see thousands of starlings. A few pairs of starlings were brought to the country many years ago. Now the bird has become a pest. The noisy starling has been joined by a cousin from Asia, a member of the same family. The *mynah* (pronounced MY-nuh) is larger than a starling, and some varieties are often sold in pet shops. This bird has spread from its normal home in Asia throughout the Pacific. Mynahs are now common in Hawaii, in the Fiji Islands, Tahiti, New Zealand and Australia.

The settlers brought in more than one animal pest, too. Many years ago someone decided there should be rabbits in Australia. The first rabbits liked the new land. By 1907 there were so many rabbits that it became necessary to build a fence 1,000 miles (1,600 kilometres) long to keep rabbits out of Western Australia. It did not succeed. Rabbits are a serious problem, although their numbers were greatly reduced by the introduction of the disease *myxomatosis*. We might say that in Australia there is a grass-eating contest between millions of kangaroos and wallabies, rabbits, sheep and cattle.

The fox, another introduction from Britain, has also thrived —at the expense of Australian sheep.

The Big Cities

If you lived in Australia, you might see some of the birds and animals we have read about. Or your home might be in one of the big, modern cities. In spite of great empty spaces on the continent, most Australians live in the cities or large towns.

Let's first visit Sydney, the birthplace of the nation and its oldest and largest city. With over 3 million people, Sydney is the fourth largest city in the British Commonwealth. Its

An aerial view of Sydney. Note the dense building and the modern expressway with its fly-over crossings

harbour is among the best, largest and most beautiful in the world. Entered through a narrow passage, the harbour widens and extends for miles. As we can see from the picture, there is a big harbour bridge; ferries go back and forth across the harbour. Ships from all over the world come to the city and it is Australia's most important port.

Because there is so much protected water, thousands of Sydney people own yachts and motor launches. Some of the best beaches are in the Sydney area.

We will read about sports and games in another section. But since surfing is Sydney's most popular sport, let's learn about this water sport now. In Sydney there are so many surfers that the local governing authority registers surfboards just as motor vehicles must be registered. There are surf clubs for adults and for children. Several surf clubs provide baby-sitters so that young mothers can enjoy the sport of riding the huge waves that come in to the beaches.

Sharks are a problem for Sydney surfers and swimmers. Each beach must have a shark patrol whose job it is to watch for sharks. Sharks usually show their fins; and when one is spotted, a member of the shark patrol begins to ring an alarm bell. When the shark alarm rings, everyone in the water heads for the beach!

Even though the water is quite cold, many people swim and ride surfboards during the winter. But it is during the Australian summer that the beaches of Sydney become most crowded. Surf carnivals are held at each beach. One important part of a

A surfboard rider

surf carnival is a lifesaving competition. Lifeguards on a Sydney beach must be well trained. The waves are almost always big and dangerous; and, as we have said, sharks are a problem. Surfing can be a dangerous sport. Riding a big wave, a surfboard may be moving at quite a speed. If the surfboard should strike a swimmer, serious injury or death could result.

Being a lifeguard on a Sydney beach is an important job and is considered an honour. Only well-trained young men are selected. Lifeguards are not paid for their services, but give them free.

Sydney is a city of beautiful parks and an outstanding zoo. One of the places boys and girls like to visit is the Koala Park in the suburbs. There are several varieties of Australian animals in the Koala Park, but it is most famous for the many koalas that may be seen.

Sydney Harbour and the famous Harbour Bridge. The white building in the centre of the picture is the new Opera House

We have read that Sydney is the capital of New South Wales. The state parliament house is in Sydney. As we can see from the pictures, there are big modern buildings in Australia's largest city. The harbour bridge is the largest single-span arch bridge in the world. The bustling harbour is the most interesting part of the city.

Sydney has one of the finest land-locked harbours in the world; it is large enough to take the entire British fleet. Splendid harbour-side suburbs spread down steep approaches to the water's edge. At week-ends in particular the harbour's sparkling waters are crowded with yachts, launches and other

58

pleasure-craft. Sydney is one of the world's most attractive cities. Its heart is Circular Quay—meeting-point for the ocean-going liners, the ferries, the trains and buses—while near by the city's spectacular development is centred around towering modern blocks. What a contrast to the scene in 1788 when Governor Phillip hoisted the Union Jack near by, on the shores of Sydney Cove, and thus founded the Colony of New South Wales!

Some Australian customs, ways of living and ways of saying things are unusual. In Sydney, council parking attendants wear brown uniforms. The people have nicknamed these attendants, who give tickets for overparking and other traffic violations, the "brown bombers".

Sydney is a bustling city. There is so much traffic that the brown bombers are kept busy. Melbourne, Australia's second largest city, has the same problem. On page 60 there is a picture of Melbourne, looking across the Yarra River which flows through the city. Melbourne people say their city is more English than any other in Australia.

Melbourne was founded in 1835 and now has nearly 3 million people. It is the capital of the state of Victoria; over half the state population lives in Melbourne. During the gold rush days, in the 1850s, thousands of new residents came to Victoria. For a time Melbourne was larger than Sydney. It was the seat of the Australian Federal Government for many years.

It is 25 miles (40 kilometres) from Melbourne to the Great Dividing Range, the mountains separating the fertile coastland from the interior. The mountains are covered with eucalyptus forests. In one area called the Dandenongs is Sherbrooke Forest, home of the beautiful lyrebird. The Healesville Sanctuary, 39 miles (62 kilometres) from Melbourne, is a famous wild animal sanctuary. Kangaroos, emus and koalas roam about inside a huge enclosure. Instead of looking at the animals through bars, visitors can walk about with the animals.

Another famous place near Melbourne is Phillip Island. There is a colony of nearly 500 koalas on Phillip Island. The whole island is a huge natural zoo. It is on Phillip Island that the fairy penguins make their nesting burrows. Each evening the famous penguin parade takes place when the birds return to land from a day of fishing far out at sea.

Melbourne is a city close to the mountains and sea. It is a

A view of Melbourne, the second largest city in Australia

Perth, the capital of Western Australia

city of beautiful parks. The Royal Botanic Gardens are the finest in the Southern Hemisphere. Captain Cook's cottage is in Fitzroy Gardens. The house was moved, piece by piece, from England and rebuilt in the park.

There is a picture on this page of another state capital city. Perth, capital of Western Australia, with an average of almost eight hours of sunshine each day, is the City of Sunshine.

We have learned that many of Australia's first settlers were convicts. Brisbane, capital of Queensland and third largest city, was established as a convict colony in 1824. This city was named after Sir Thomas Brisbane, one of the early governors of New South Wales, in the days before Queensland was a separate colony. Brisbane was descended from Scotsman Robert Bruce and the kings of Scotland.

61

A view of the harbour of Tasmania's capital, Hobart

However, many of Australia's finest citizens are descendants of convicts. Many of the convicts who were responsible for establishing the great cities of Australia were no longer interested in a life of crime. They welcomed the chance to begin new lives and were willing to work hard. But there were others who were not interested in becoming good citizens. Tasmania and its capital, Hobart, were settled by convicts. Many of these escaped, and found that it was possible to live in the bush, hunting wild birds and animals for food.

The escaped convicts (known as bushrangers) sometimes attacked travellers and the homes of free settlers. Later, escaped convicts and others on the mainland of Australia became bushrangers, too. You have probably heard of the famous Kelly gang, who once captured a whole town. We can compare the bushrangers with the gangs of robbers and gunslingers who sometimes attacked settlements and ranches in the Wild West of America.

While Australia's history is in some respects like that of the United States, and while Australians are said to have adopted many American ways, the customs are still, in the main, English. Cars are driven on the left; Australians, like Englishmen, like their afternoon tea. And—they like cricket. The periodic Test series between the two countries for the honour of carrying home or retaining the mythical "Ashes" is sufficient proof of this.

Australia's Farmers

Although over four fifths of Australia's population lives in cities, Australia is an important farming country. We have already read that there are more sheep raised in Australia than in any other country. The sheep number over 136,000,000! It is interesting that Australia's neighbour, New Zealand, although much smaller in area and in population, exports more meat than any other nation. Lamb and mutton are New Zealand's most important meat export.

Australia produces and exports much meat too. There are about 26,000,000 head of cattle in the country. But wool is its most important product. About one quarter of all the world's

Sheep, in large numbers, are always a familiar sight in some areas of Australia. This flock is part of a total sheep population larger than that of any other country in the world

Wheat harvesting—wheat is an important crop in Australia today

wool clip (sheared wool) comes from Australia. Some sixty per cent of all the world's production of merino wool comes from Australia. There are different varieties of sheep, and the merino is one that grows especially fine wool.

We have read about the great waterless sections of central Australia. There are other parts of the country either too mountainous or covered with jungle to make farming possible. Fifty-five per cent of all the land area is suitable only for pasture.

However, there are parts of Australia where farmers grow wheat and oats, sugar-cane and cotton, maize and rice, fruits, hops and tobacco. Australia is the eighth country in the world in producing wheat, and third biggest of the wheat exporters.

The picture on page 65 shows us that wheat fields are large and that Australian farmers use modern equipment in harvesting their crops. This picture was taken in the state of Victoria where there are important wheat-growing areas.

Cotton is an increasingly important crop in parts of New South Wales. Sugar-cane has long been one of Queensland's most important crops. Tobacco is grown in Victoria, Queensland and Western Australia. And there are fruit orchards in all the states. The little island state of Tasmania is the most important fruit-producing area.

Tasmania's fruit farms are usually small, while the wheat, cattle and sheep farmers may own great tracts of land.

Fruit-growing in Tasmania is a family business. The whole family, boys and girls included, help—especially during harvest time. Tasmanian apples are grown to be eaten by Australians and also for export. One of the important varieties of apples grown for export has a peculiar name. It is called the "Democrat".

There are vineyards in several parts of Australia, notably around the lower reaches of the Murray River and in the Hunter Valley of New South Wales. Australian wines are excellent.

Along the Derwent Valley of Tasmania are fine hop farms; hops are also grown in Victoria.

We have said that Australians like their cup of tea. But the national drink is beer, which is made from hops. The hop is a vine. It is a member of the mulberry family. It has been culti-

Picking apples of the "Golden Delicious" variety in Tasmania

vated in Europe for hundreds of years. The leafy flower clusters are gathered, dried, then used in brewing.

If we are to be precise, we should say the plant is called hop. The dried flower clusters used in making beer are called hops. The hop was first cultivated in England in 1525; by 1629 it was being grown in the American colonies. Tasmanian hops are among the largest found in cultivation, and the hop crop is very important in the island state. Hop farmers, like fruit-growers, usually have small farms.

As we have said, Australian farmers have modern farming equipment. Farm homes are comfortable. Farmers who grow fruits, or hops, or who have vineyards usually own farms that

67

would be considered quite small in a country such as America, but by contrast there are many huge sheep and cattle stations.

We often read that Australians use the word *mob* for a large group of animals! They speak of a mob of sheep, cattle or kangaroos. Instead of a roundup of sheep or a roundup of cattle the word used is *muster*. The men who do the mustering, and look after the sheep and cattle at other times, are usually called *stockmen*. Only in Australia and New Zealand are these words used in connection with cattle and sheep raising. There are other unusual expressions used on the stations, too. A bed roll is called a *swag*. An Australian who steals or rustles cattle is called a *poddy-dodger*.

There are many big sheep stations in New South Wales. Some stations are near enough to towns for the station family and hands to go in for shopping, or to the cinema. The station family usually has modern conveniences, including refrigeration, electric light and a family car.

However, there are stations in western New South Wales and other parts of Australia which are far away from the nearest town, or even the nearest neighbour. Let's visit a typical Outback cattle station and learn about mustering, stockmen and poddy-dodgers.

Visit to a Cattle Station

Life on an Outback station is much like life on a Western cattle range in America about 75 years ago. Neighbours may be far distant. A visit to town may take place once a month, perhaps only once a year. Of course station people in the Outback are modern so far as circumstances allow. The station usually has a two-way radio so that it may communicate with other stations, with police stations in case of trouble, and with the Flying Doctor Service in case of illness.

There is electricity, provided by a generator. The station family usually has a Land Rover. Many stations have landing strips and some have private planes.

Stockmen sometimes ride out to the cattle on motorcycles but for most of his work the stockman still relies on his horse. When mustering and driving cattle, he may spend days in the saddle and many nights sleeping around a campfire.

The cattle may be driven to the nearest railway or port for shipment. Or it may be necessary to drive them from one range to another for better grazing.

First, the stockmen muster the cattle from the far corners of the station. Except in the stockyards, a lasso is not used. Instead, the stockman rides alongside a steer, jumps off his horse and grabs the steer's tail. Then he forces the steer to the ground by twisting its tail.

Cattle raised on stations in parts of Western Australia or in the Northern Territory must often be driven long distances to new ranges in Queensland. This is done during the months when no rain falls and the Outback country dries up completely. If cattle are ready for market, the mob may be driven to The Alice for shipment by rail to Adelaide. Or the mob may be driven through the bush of the Northern Territory to Darwin and then shipped by sea to some overseas market.

Whatever the reason, driving several thousand or even several hundred head of cattle is a long, hot and sometimes dangerous job. A kangaroo suddenly dashing into the mob may cause a stampede, known in Australia as a *rush*. Water is a treasure for both stockmen and cattle. If a water hole is found dry, or a windmill over a deep well is found broken, men and animals may die of thirst. However, cattle are increasingly being moved not on their own hooves but by road transport and huge trucks with long trains of trailers are now a feature of outback roads.

The aborigines are important hands on a cattle station. We have read about their ability to find water and travel in the Outback country without becoming lost. Some of the best cattle hands are aborigines. There are times when only an

A herd of cattle being driven across a river in Queensland

aborigine stockman is able to stop a stampede. The stockman begins to sing an aboriginal song in a low voice. As he sings the bellowing and restless cattle begin to become quiet. In a matter of minutes a mob of cattle about to stampede are once again quiet and willing to move in the right direction.

We have read about interesting animals, many of which are found in the Outback. During the long cattle drive the mob may pass by mobs of brumbies, the wild horses of the north. There are many wild cattle also. And there are hundreds of wild camels, descended from the animals used by early explorers, and by Afghan traders. Until the railway from Adelaide to Alice Springs was completed in 1929, many cattle stations received their supplies by camel train. There were

Afghan traders (natives of Afghanistan in Asia) who visited the isolated stations with their camel caravans.

The Australians who operate the Outback cattle stations lead pioneer lives. The climate is not pleasant, with weeks of terrible heat. Obtaining good water may often become a problem during long dry seasons. Kangaroos and dingoes must be hunted; rabbits kept under control. There are poddy-dodgers who will steal cattle from parts of the station that are far from the station headquarters.

For many station people a visit to neighbours is impossible. Even visiting the nearest town to buy supplies is hard work.

In addition to a Land Rover, a caravan may be used if the station family must travel a long distance. Along highways there are special caravan camps with water available so that travellers can spend the night. An Outback family thinks nothing of driving 150 miles (240 kilometres) to a town.

However, families in the Outback are never really far from one another or from help in time of trouble. We have read that the two-way radio is an important piece of equipment. The radio is used in time of illness, either to get advice from a doctor or to call the doctor. More and more landing strips are being built for small planes. Commercial air services are also getting better and better. The settlements in the Outback are connected by air with the big cities. A family can, if it desires, drive a medium distance, board a modern airliner and visit one of Australia's big cities within a few hours.

It is the two-way radio that is still the most important link

Australian children in school

between Outback people, their neighbours and settlements. If you lived in the Outback, you might go to school in your own home. Your teacher might be several hours' drive away. The teacher and the pupil talk together over the two-way radio. Homework is given, questions are asked and answered, tests given—all by radio.

It would be interesting to go to school in this way, wouldn't it? Of course most boys and girls in Australia go to school just as you do.

Schools, Games and Sports

Education is free and compulsory. By this we mean that, as in all civilised countries, children must attend school. Unless they attend a private school, there is no cost. Going to school in Australia is much like going to school in our country. Boys and girls study the same subjects. Since Australia is south of the equator, the summer holidays begin a little time before Christmas.

Boys at the King's School

Australian tennis-players— many of the world-champions come from Australia

We have learned that children living in the Outback go to school by radio. The School of the Air began in 1950, with headquarters at Alice Springs. This method of teaching was so successful that other Schools of the Air were established in the Outback parts of South Australia and New South Wales. Many children living in isolated areas also study by post. Or sometimes the School of the Air and a correspondence course are combined.

We have said that Australians follow many English customs but also have their own ways of doing things. In the southern states, they have developed a game of their own called Australian Rules football. This game, which combines some of the features of rugby, soccer and Irish football, originated on the goldfields of Victoria. There are several leagues. A grand final at the Melbourne Cricket Ground will draw

110,000 people. The season for this fast, open variety of football is from April to September.

Australians are good swimmers and tennis players, too. Each year world championships are won by young swimmers from Australia. In tennis, Australians' success as Davis Cup winners dates back to 1907 and includes an unbroken run of victories from 1959 to 1963. In that year the Cup was lost to the U.S.A., only to be regained in 1964. Australia has also produced a good many Wimbledon champions, both men and women. Australian players always take part in international tennis tournaments and are usually among the winners.

Horse racing is another sport with many followers. As many as 50,000 to 60,000 people attend a big race. There are race courses in all large cities. The Melbourne Cup Race draws 100,000 people.

Horse-racing events like this one are popular in Australia

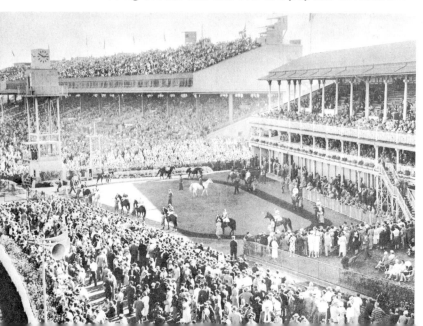

Playing bowls in Sydney, with the Harbour Bridge in the background

Australians certainly enjoy games and sports and are very good at practically all kinds of sports, but they also work hard at such serious things as government.

About the Government

From 1788, when the first convict settlement was established by Captain Phillip at Sydney Cove, until 1839, most Australian settlers were ex-convicts. Transportation of criminals from Britain gradually stopped after 1839, but it was the gold strikes in the 1850s that began large-scale settlement. The government at this time was similar to that in the American colonies. There were a number of separate colonies, each with its own colonial government. It is interesting that for many years New Zealand, although 1,200 miles (1,920 kilometres) away, was considered a part of the colony of New South Wales.

The six colonies of Australia remained separate until 1901 when they became federated or joined together.

The powers entrusted to the Federal Government and those retained by the States (formerly colonies) were strictly defined in a written Constitution. Broadly speaking, the Federal Government laws cover those fields where central power is preferable—defence, foreign affairs, taxation, posts and telegraphs, Customs and excise, protection of shipping, meteorological services and so on. State Governments retain power in such fields as education and ownership of land. Where it is impracticable for either Federal or State Government to act alone there is division of powers. The States are proud of their individual rights and powers. On occasions when the Federal Government has sought to alter the Constitution (unforeseen developments can make such changes desirable or even essential) this has almost always been refused by the electors, who

The War Memorial in Canberra—the beautiful yellow flowers are the flowers of the spring wattle plant

are entitled to vote on such matters. It would seem that a written Constitution, instead of an unwritten one like Britain's, can cause its own problems.

Australia's system of government by an elected parliament is based largely on that of Britain. However, the statesmen who hammered out Australia's federal system borrowed certain ideas from the United States.

Australia's lower House, the House of Representatives, is the equivalent of Britain's House of Commons. It has 125 Members, each elected for a three-year term.

The upper House, the Senate, is unlike Britain's House of Lords (peers are not, of course, elected). Senators, like Members of the House of Representatives, are elected by the people, and there are ten Senators for each State. Each Senator is elected for six years, with half the Senators retiring at the end of each three-year term. The Senate, like the House of Lords, is a house of review, with the power to veto any proposed law (except bills relating to finance) sent up to it from "the other place". This power is used only in a real emergency.

The Australian system of government, like the British, is a carefully devised system of checks and balances aimed at preventing abuse of power.

At the head of the Australian system is the British Sovereign's direct representative, the Governor-General, who is theoretically in supreme control. Most of his functions are formal but he can, in emergency, veto any proposed measures of the Australian Parliament.

As in Britain, the Prime Minister must dissolve Parliament if the Government is defeated in the House by a vote of no-confidence. The Governor-General then decides, with advice from the various parliamentary leaders, whether an alternative Government—perhaps a coalition—can be formed or whether an election must be held.

Over the years since federation, Australian governments have passed a series of laws that give Australians what some people call a *welfare state*. By this we mean that, as in the United Kingdom, the government provides many services that are provided by private business in other countries. In Australia the government pays the greater part of the cost of medicines needed by its citizens. Much of the cost of medical care and hospitalization is paid by the government. The government pays for old age, war and invalid pensions. The blind and people who have tuberculosis also receive pensions. All mothers receive a special payment for children. This child endowment continues up to the age of 16, or until the age of 21 if the child continues with full-time studies.

The government of a country is administered from its capital city. In 1911 Australians decided to build a new capital, to be located in the Australian Capital Territory. The area selected lies in the state of New South Wales, south of Sydney and north of Melbourne, capital of Victoria. The capital city was named Canberra. A worldwide competition among architects was held to select a plan for the new capital city. An American architect from Chicago won the competition. Australia's beautiful capital was planned by Mr. Walter Burley Griffin.

Canberra, with a population now about 250,000 is the most rapidly growing city, for its size, in Australia. It is a beautiful city with lovely parks, wide streets and—most recently added feature—a big artificial lake which has been named after the city's designer. As well as Parliament House, which is the centre for Australia's government, Canberra is the home of a beautiful Australian War Memorial, the National Library, the National University, Royal Military College, Australian Academy of Science, and many other modern buildings.

As in other British Commonwealth countries, the British Government is represented by a Governor-General. The Prime Minister reports important events to this representative of the British Crown. When the government loses in a no-confidence vote, it is the representative of the Crown who dissolves Parliament and calls for new elections. The Australian government is really quite independent of Britain. But there is great loyalty to Britain, which keeps some old customs alive. The Australian flag, like that of New Zealand, includes the Union Jack to show the relationship between the Commonwealth and Britain. The Union Jack is in the top left corner. The ground colour is blue with a large seven-pointed star under the Union Jack and the stars of the Southern Cross on the right. The Southern Cross is a constellation of stars seen daily in the Southern Hemisphere. The flags of Australia and New Zealand are quite similar. Both have a blue field, and both have stars.

The relationships between Australia and Britain are shown

The Academy of Science, Canberra

in numerous other ways. Envelopes containing official government business are marked ON HER MAJESTY'S SERVICE. The Australian Navy is called the Royal Australian Navy.

But we have also learned that Australians have developed ways of speech and ways of doing things that are truly Australian. Australians call themselves Aus-TRY-lee-ans, which is their own pronunciation, not the British way of saying the name. The influence of the United States is also seen in speech and in customs. Since World War II, Australians have seen that their future security lies in closer relationships with the United States.

Before World War II, Australia counted on Britain to defend her in time of trouble. And Australians loyally supported

Britain when the mother country was in trouble. But in 1942 the British colony of Hong Kong was captured by the Japanese. Then Singapore, considered a fortress and a naval base that could not possibly be taken, was captured by the Japanese. Tens of thousands of Australian soldiers (and soldiers of New Zealand too) were killed or captured or found themselves far away from home, serving alongside British troops in the battle against the Germans. Darwin, capital of the Northern Territory and the most important port in the north, was heavily bombed by Japanese planes. Australia found herself under air attack, threatened by a powerful enemy; and the protection of the British Army, Navy and Air Force was gone. Suddenly Australia and the United States became allies because the United States was fighting the same enemy in the Pacific.

Industries and Culture

Australia's manufacturing industries were forced to expand and achieve high efficiency by the needs of the Second World War. Some quite new industries came into being. Australia had to make her own tanks, aeroplanes, high-precision optical equipment and a wide range of other things which in pre-war years would have seemed quite beyond the nation's ability.

Since the war, factories have continued to expand and diversify. Today Australian factories produce most of the goods needed by a modern country—motor vehicles, electronic equipment, petro-chemicals. Australian shipyards build ocean-going vessels. A highly efficient steel industry provides the raw material for a wide range of heavy industries fully capable of producing such items as diesel electric locomotives and heavy earth-moving equipment.

And although Australia still relies mainly on the export of rural products—very particularly, wool—to earn income

Although Australia is so well-known for her agriculture, her industries do not lag behind. This plant is not untypical

abroad, she is increasingly exporting factory products to supplement her overseas earnings, as well as very large quantities of minerals. Indeed, Australia is now one of the world's main exporters of minerals, especially to such industrial countries as Japan and South Korea.

In cultural fields as well as industrial ones, Australians are gaining much overseas attention. For years past Australian singers, for example, have earned fame abroad. One of the earliest and best known was the late Dame Nellie Melba. Of present-day famous Australian singers, perhaps the best-known is Joan Sutherland. More recent has been the marked success of Australian painters—such as Sidney Nolan. Many Australian writers are now internationally known; Patrick White is one of the many whose books have more than mere local appeal. He was awarded a Nobel Prize in 1974.

Australia's Problems

Australia is a very large country. One of the problems is that too much of the land is wild, dry and still partly unexplored. It is essential for sources of water to be developed, if the great Outback areas are to be put to use. We have learned that many areas are desert, and have so little water that farming is not possible. Parts of this desert area could be reclaimed with irrigation. However, in the salt pan areas where some of the aborigines live, all the topsoil is gone so that even water will not make it fertile. Other vast areas lack only water in order to support prosperous communities.

In solving some of these problems, Australia is creating new ones. Although it has been an independent member of the British family of nations since 1901, Australians have been loyal to the British Crown. The people of Australia have developed their own customs, but they have also held to many customs of the old country.

Despite the fact that Australia is geographically within the south-east Asia region and is becoming increasingly a trade partner with south-east Asian countries, most Australians feel that, like many Asian countries, they should decide who shall immigrate and in what numbers. This has given rise to talk of a "White Australia Policy". In fact, such a policy has never officially existed, and now does not exist even unofficially. Moreover, under the Colombo Plan and similar international schemes, Australia has played a large part in educating thousands of students from south-east Asian countries, to fit them for the task of improving living standards and conditions in their homelands.

Vast numbers of immigrants have come to Australia during

A view of Lake Eucumbene, now part of the Snowy Mountains Scheme

the last thirty years, only some of the newcomers have been British. The rest have been Italians, Hungarians, Poles—non-English-speaking people from all over Europe—as well as an increasingly large number from other continents. Australia now accepts immigrants from more than one hundred countries.

Australia's new citizens are changing the country and its customs. When I was travelling in the Outback country of the Northern Territory, my driver was a Greek. He had learned to speak English, and married an Australian girl. Other new citizens are refugees from the countries of Eastern Europe which are now Communist-controlled.

In order to provide new farming land and new jobs for more and more immigrants, the Australian government is building great dams to create reservoirs to hold the rain that does fall. A reservoir not only holds water; the water can be used to produce electricity for new settlements, for new farms and for new factories.

Australia's Snowy Mountains Scheme has been described as one of the five modern wonders of the world. We have learned that the Snowy Mountains are a part of the Great Dividing Range separating the coastal area from the dry middle of Australia. There is heavy rainfall on the eastern slopes of the Snowy Mountains. The Snowy River system, which flows into the Tasman Sea, carries enough water for a great deal of irrigation; but in order to use the water, engineers had to make it flow backward, or from east to west. The project was costly and unusual because great tunnels had to be dug through the mountains so that when the scheme was completed water would flow into the relatively dry country west of the Great Dividing Range. Even though the Snowy Mountains Scheme was started in 1949, it was not completed until 1973. The final cost was about $A800 million.

Now the Snowy Mountains Scheme is complete, there are 100 miles (160 kilometres) of tunnels. Aqueducts have been built to carry water into inland areas. There are nine big dams and many smaller dams to hold the rainfall in reservoirs.

The Snowy Mountains Scheme needed so many workers and engineers that the Australian government established a special immigration department to find skilled workers and men of technical training. People from 30 different nations have been employed in the project.

Much of the construction work was in uninhabited bush country. In order to begin the project, it was necessary to build new roads. Supplies were delivered to remote construction camps by parachute. A special radio network connected all the many camps.

As the Australian government seeks and finds new citizens, it is providing new land for its newcomers. The electricity produced in the underground power stations is being fed to new farms, new settlements, and new factories that have been built. We can understand why this unusual project has been called one of the future wonders of the world.

A Snowy Mountains power station far underground

Three things have changed Australian thinking and ways of life. First is that during the Second World War Britain, fully involved on the other side of the world, was no longer able to give Australia the protection and help she needed. Australians were obliged, especially when Japan entered the war and sent powerful forces into the South Pacific, to turn to the United States for security. Thousands of Americans and Australians served together in the Pacific region during the war. There was

91

also close post-war co-operation. Australia, New Zealand and the United States have signed a military treaty: the Anzus Pact.

Secondly, about half of all immigrants to Australia in post-war years have come from non-English-speaking countries. They have brought new customs, new ways of life. They have been a very refreshing influence.

Thirdly, Australia is no longer far away from the rest of the world. Modern jet planes take Australians abroad. Even London—almost the furthest spot on the globe from Sydney—can be reached in about thirty-six hours. Australia's old sense of being remote from the world is breaking down.

Although the Australian Government have relaxed their restrictions on Asian immigrants, the whole question of relationships with Asia is being carefully examined, largely due to increasing trade with Asian countries and particularly Japan. Australians are anxious to help neighbouring lands develop along democratic paths. This is why Australia is fully active in such organisations as the South-East Asia Treaty Organisation and in the South Pacific Commission, aimed at helping the smaller, less developed communities of the area towards development and self-government.

Index

93

rabbits 54, 72
rainfall 13, 16, 18
rice 16, 65

salt pan areas 27, 87
schools 30, 32, 72–3, 74–5
seasons 13, 18
Senate 80
sharks 19, 56–7
sheep 15, 16, 33, 37, 38, 64–5, 68
shipbuilding 85
skiing 18
skin-diving 20
Snowy Mountains 16, 89
Snowy Mountains irrigation scheme
89–90
Snowy River 89
Solomon Islands 12, 22
South Australia 17, 21, 39, 75
S.E.A.T.O. 92
State Governments 30, 79
stations 16
Stuart, John McDouall 35, 39, 40
sugar 65–6
surfing 18, 56–7
Sutherland, Joan 86
swimming 56–7, 76
Sydney 18, 20, 36, 37, 49, 55–9, 78

Tasman, Captain Abel 36
Tasman Sea 12, 36, 90
Tasmania 12, 16, 17, 18, 36, 37, 62, 66

telegraph line 39
Temperate Zone 16
Tennant Creek 40
tennis 76
Timor Sea 12
tobacco 65–6
Torres Strait 12
Torrid Zone 13
tropics 13
two-way radio 32, 40, 69, 72–3

United Nations 22
United States of America 84, 92

Victoria 17, 20, 37, 66, 75
vineyards 66

walkabout 33
wallabies 16, 31, 44–5
Warburton, P. E. 39
welfare state 81
Western Australia 15, 17, 18, 21,
37, 61, 66, 70
wheat 16, 65–6
White, Patrick 86
Wills, William John 39
wombat 51
wool 37, 64–5
woomera 28–9, 34
World War II 12, 22, 83, 91

Yarra River 59

95